Little Pebble™

T0081107

Mammals in the Wild

Bottlenose Dolphins

by Kathryn Clay

PEBBLE
a capstone imprint

Pebble Books are published by Pebble
1710 Roe Crest Drive, North Mankato,
Minnesota 56003
www.capstonepub.com

Copyright © 2019 by Pebble, a Capstone imprint.
All rights reserved. No part of this publication may be reproduced in whole or in part, or stored in a retrieval system, or transmitted in any form or by any means, electronic, mechanical, photocopying, recording, or otherwise, without written permission of the publisher.

Library of Congress Cataloging-in-Publication Data
Names: Clay, Kathryn, author.
Title: Bottlenose dolphins : / by Kathryn Clay.
Description: North Mankato, Minnesota : an imprint of Pebble, [2019] Series: Little Pebble. Mammals in the wild | Audience: Age 4–7.
Identifiers: LCCN 2018004129 (print) | LCCN 2018009132 (ebook) | ISBN 9781977100894 (eBook PDF) | ISBN 9781977100771 (hardcover) | ISBN 9781977100832 (paperback)
Subjects: LCSH: Bottlenose dolphin—Juvenile literature.
Classification: LCC QL737.C432 (ebook) | LCC QL737.C432 C555 2019 (print) | DDC 599.53/3—dc23
LC record available at https://lccn.loc.gov/2018004129

Editorial Credits
Karen Aleo, editor; Juliette Peters, designer;
Tracy Cummins and Heather Mauldin, media researchers;
Laura Manthe, production specialist

Photo Credits
Getty Images: David J Slater, 11; iStockphoto: BrettCharlton, 15, shironosov, 19; Shutterstock: Croisy, 1, Gerald Marella, Cover, 7, likemuzzy, Design Element, Matt A. Claiborne, 13, Matt9122, 9, Tory Kallman, 5, 17, Val_Iva, Design Element, vkilikov, 21

Printed in the United States 5489

Table of Contents

At Sea 4

In the Wild 8

Baby Dolphins 20

Glossary 22
Read More 23
Internet Sites 23
Critical Thinking Questions . . 24
Index 24

At Sea

Splash!

A bottlenose dolphin is here.

It jumps.

Hi!

Dolphins live in warm water.

They live in the ocean.

In the Wild

Dolphins swim fast.

Tails help them swim.

Flippers help them turn.

Go!

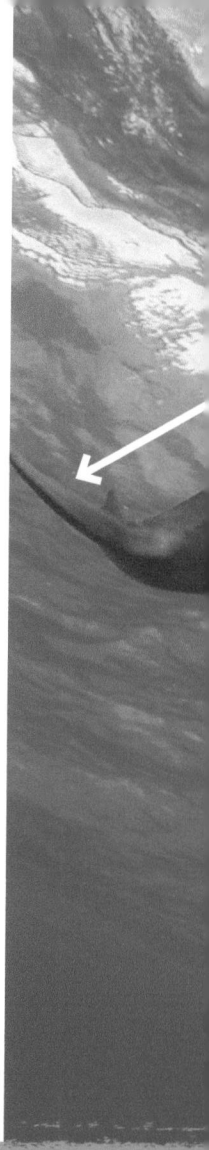

tail
flippers

Dolphins find food.

They eat fish.

Yum!

Dolphins have a long mouth.

It is called a beak.

They have many teeth.

Dolphins are mammals.

They come up for air.

They use a blowhole.

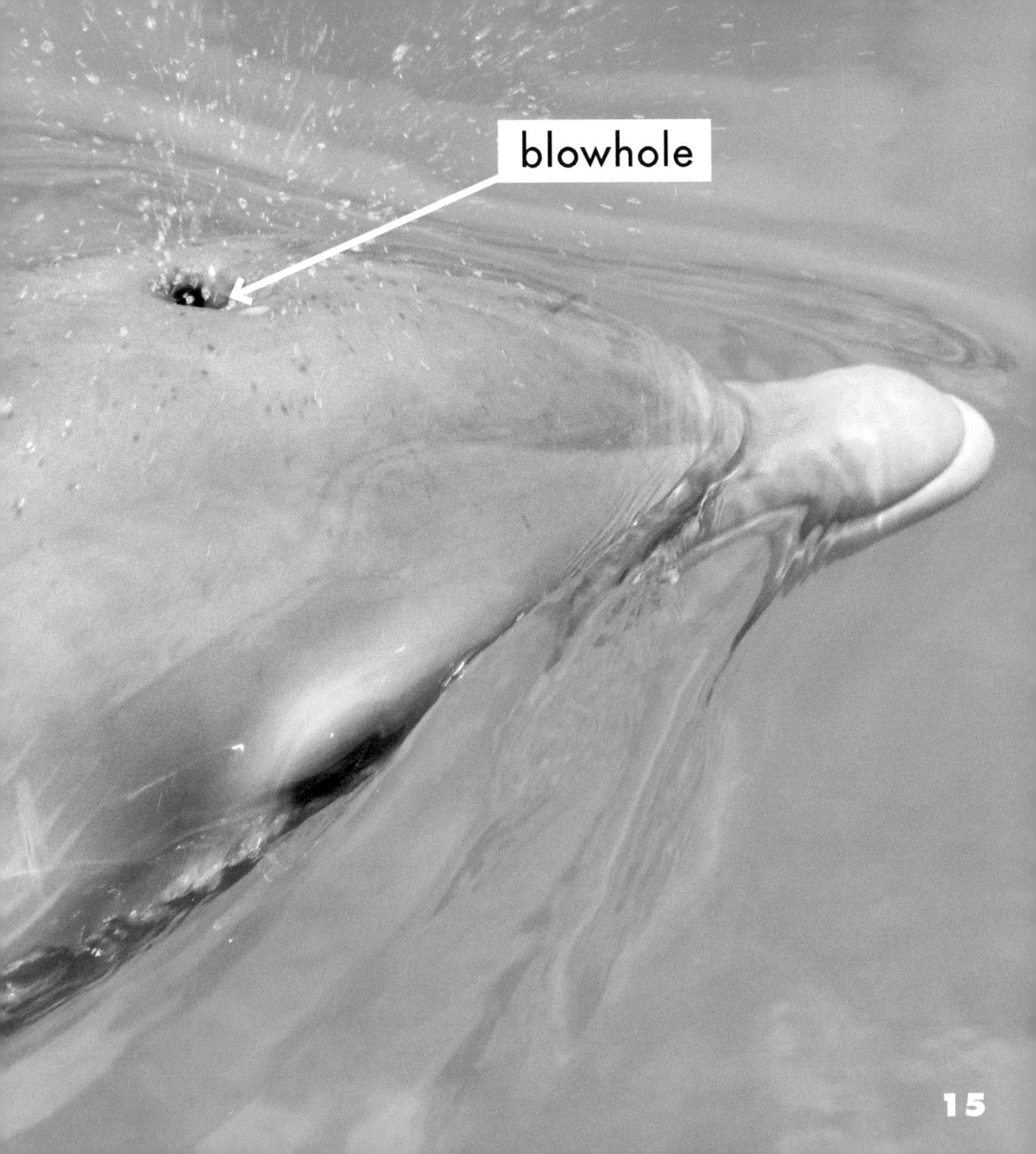
blowhole

Dolphins swim together.

This is caled a pod.

Look at them go!

Squeak.

Dolphins talk to each other.

Baby Dolphins

A calf is born.

It drinks milk.

It swims too.

Glossary

beak—the long front part of a dolphin's head that includes the jaws

blowhole—a hole on top of a dolphin's head; dolphins breathe air through blowholes

calf—a young dolphin

flipper—one of the broad, flat limbs of a sea creature

mammal—a warm-blooded animal that breathes air; mammals have hair or fur; female mammals feed milk to their young

ocean—a large body of salt water

pod—a group of dolphins

tail—the part at the back end of an animal's body

Read More

Hansen, Grace. *Bottlenose Dolphins.* Animal Friends. Minneapolis: Abdo Kids, 2016.

Macdhui, Lori. *How Do Dolphins Communicate?* How Life Science Works. New York: PowerKids Press, 2018.

Statts, Leo. *Dolphins.* Zoom in on Ocean Animals. Minneapolis: Abdo Zoom, 2017.

Internet Sites

Use FactHound to find Internet sites related to this book.

Visit www.facthound.com

Just type in 9781977100771 and go.

Check out projects, games and lots more at **www.capstonekids.com**

Critical Thinking Questions

1. How might flippers help dolphins swim?
2. What do dolphins eat?
3. How do dolphins breathe?

Index

beaks, 12
blowholes, 14
calves, 20
fish, 10
flippers, 8
jumping, 4,
mammals, 14
milk, 20
oceans, 6
pods, 16
swimming, 8, 16, 20
tails, 8
talking, 18
teeth, 12